Y Gerddoriaeth Hynaf
The Oldest Music
An Ceol is Sine

Phil Cope

T0163133

Barddoniaeth a ysbrydolwyd gan ffynhonnau sanctaidd Llwch Garmon a Phenfro

gan gynnwys gweithiau hen a newydd gan Lewys Glyn Cothi, Gwynfardd Brycheiniog, Ieuan ap Rhydderch, Angela Graham, Tony Curtis, Grace O'Reilly, Eirwyn George, Dafydd Williams, Julian Cason, Lorraine O'Dwyer, Brian Jackson, Phil Carradice a Phil Cope

a ffotograffau Phil Cope

Cyfrol 1 yn y gyfres:
Ffynhonnau Sanctaidd Llwch Garmon a Phenfro

Cysylltiadau Hynafol | Llwybrau Pererindod Llwch Garmon a Phenfro | Parthian Books

---

Poetry inspired by the sacred springs and holy wells of Wexford and Pembrokeshire

including old and new works by Lewys Glyn Cothi, Gwynfardd Brycheiniog, Ieuan ap Rhydderch, Angela Graham, Tony Curtis, Grace O'Reilly, Eirwyn George, Dafydd Williams, Julian Cason, Lorraine O'Dwyer, Brian Jackson, Phil Carradice and Phil Cope

with the photographs of Phil Cope

Volume 1 in the series:
Holy Wells of Wexford and Pembrokeshire

Ancient Connections | Wexford-Pembrokeshire Pilgrim Way | Parthian Books

---

Filíocht spreagtha ag fuaráin naofa agus toibreacha beannaithe Loch Garman agus Sir Benfro

lena n-áirítear saothair, idir shean agus nua, le Lewys Glyn Cothi, Gwynfardd Brycheiniog, Ieuan ap Rhydderch, Angela Graham, Tony Curtis, Grace O'Reilly, Eirwyn George, Dafydd Williams, Julian Cason, Lorraine O'Dwyer, Brian Jackson, Phil Carradice agus Phil Cope

maille le grianghraif le Phil Cope

Imleabhar 1 sa tsraith:
Toibreacha Beannaithe Loch Garman agus Sir Benfro

Ceangal Ársa | Bealach Oilithreachta Loch Garman agus Sir Benfro | Parthian Books

CYMRAEG

Cyfrol 1 yn y gyfres:
Ffynhonnau Sanctaidd Llwch Garmon a Phenfro

Mae ffynhonnell ddibynadwy o ddŵr glân yn hanfodol i unrhyw gymuned, felly nid yw'n anodd deall pwysigrwydd ffynhonnau i bobloedd cyn-fodern. Yr hyn sy'n fwy cymhleth yw'r berthynas gyfriniol mae dynol ryw wedi'i datblygu â'r safleoedd hyn a ystyriwyd yn rhai cysegredig hyd yn oed cyn dyfodiad Cristnogaeth. Cyfres o bum llyfryn sy'n dathlu ffynhonnau sanctaidd mewn dwy ardal â hynafiaeth a hanes cyffredin yw *Ffynhonnau Sanctaidd Llwch Garmon a Phenfro*. Ers yr Oes Efydd ac efallai ynghynt, bu teithio dros y môr rhwng y ddwy wlad yn fodd o rannu traddodiadau ac enwau cyffredin sy'n gysylltiedig â ffynhonnau'r ddwy ardal. Mae'r hen gyfeillgarwch rhwng dau sant Cristnogol cynnar yn arwyddocaol hefyd: Dewi a ddaeth yn Esgob cyntaf ar Dyddewi; ac Aeddan a aned yn Iwerddon ond a dreuliodd amser yng Nghymru cyn sefydlu mynachlogydd yn Iwerddon, gan gynnwys un yn Ninas Gwernin. Mae ffynnon wedi'i chysegru i Dewi yn Bearna na hAille (Oilgate), Llwch Garmon ac mae ffynnon wedi'i henwi ar ôl Aeddan ym Mhorth Mawr ger Tyddewi. Mae pob un o'r pum llyfryn yn ymdrin â'r pwnc o safbwynt gwahanol, gan gynnwys ffuglen, barddoniaeth ac ysgrifau yn ogystal â ffotograffau a phrintiau.

Lluniwyd y gyfrol hon, *Y Gerddoriaeth Hynaf*, gan Phil Cope, ffotograffydd ac awdur o dde Cymru sydd wedi cyhoeddi nifer o weithiau am ffynhonnau sanctaidd. Yma, trwy ddetholiad o gerddi hen a newydd, yn Gymraeg, Saesneg a Gwyddeleg, a'i ffotograffau hudolus ei hun, mae Phil Cope yn archwilio sut y mae ffynhonnau sanctaidd wedi ysbrydoli beirdd ers canrifoedd.

ENGLISH

Volume 1 in the series:
Holy Wells of Wexford and Pembrokeshire

A reliable and clean source of water is essential for any community, so it is easy to understand how important wells were for pre-modern peoples. More complex is the mystical relationship humans have developed with these sites, which are imbued with a sacredness that predates Christianity. *Holy Wells of Wexford and Pembrokeshire* is a series of five chapbooks celebrating holy wells in two regions with common ancestry and history. Since at least the Bronze Age, sea travel between these two lands has meant cross fertilisation of traditions and common names associated with wells of both regions. Of significance is the long-standing friendship between two early Christian saints: David, who became the first Bishop of St Davids; and Aidan, born in Ireland, who spent time in Wales and then founded monasteries in Ireland, including at Ferns. In Oilgate, Wexford, there is a well dedicated to David and, at Whitesands near St Davids in Pembrokeshire, there is one named after Aidan. Each of the five books approaches the subject from a different perspective, including fiction, poetry and essays as well as photographs and prints.

This volume, *The Oldest Music*, has been compiled by Phil Cope, a photographer and author based in south Wales who has several published works on the subject of holy wells. It explores and celebrates how holy wells have inspired poets for hundreds of years and includes a selection of old and new poems, in Welsh, English and Irish, illustrated by Phil Cope's compelling photographs.

GAEILGE

Imleabhar 1 sa tsraith:
Toibreacha Beannaithe Loch Garman agus Sir Benfro

Bunriachtanas do phobal ar bith foinse ghlan iontaofa uisce, mar sin is furasta a thuiscint a thábhachtaí a bhí toibreacha do lucht an tseansaoil. Rud níos casta is ea an ceangal misteach a d'fhorbair idir daoine agus na háiteanna seo lena mbaineann naofacht is sine ná an Chríostaíocht. Sraith cúig leabhrán é *Toibreacha Beannaithe Loch Garman agus Sir Benfro*, sraith ina ndéantar céiliúradh ar na toibreacha beannaithe atá sa dá réigiún sin ag a bhfuil oidhreacht agus stair choiteann. Ón gCré-umhaois i leith, ar a laghad, de bharr na dturas farraige idir an dá réigiún, cros-síolraíodh agus scaipeadh seanchas agus cáil na ndaoine a luaití leis na toibreacha sin. Tá tábhacht ar leith leis an gcairdeas buan idir beirt naomh den Luath-Chríostaíocht: Dáibhí, céad easpag Tyddewi; agus Aodhán, a rugadh in Éirinn, a chaith seal sa Bhreatain Bheag agus a bhunaigh mainistreacha in Éirinn, ceann i bhFearna san áireamh. I Maolán na nGabhar, Contae Loch Garman, tiomnaíodh tobar beannaithe do Dháibhí agus in aice Porth Mawr in Sir Benfro ainmníodh tobar eile as Aodhán. Téann gach leabhrán i ngleic leis an ábhar ar bhealach éagsúil – ficsean, filíocht, aistí, grianghraif agus priontaí uile san áireamh.

San imleabhar seo, *An Ceol is Sine*, déantar iniúchadh agus céiliúradh ar an inspioráid a thug toibreacha beannaithe d'fhilí leis na cianta. Tá rogha dánta ann, idir shean agus nua, i mBreatnais, i mBéarla agus i nGaeilge, maille le grianghraif mhealltacha Phil Cope, grianghrafadóir agus údar atá lonnaithe i ndeisceart na Breataine Bige agus a d'fhoilsigh roinnt saothar roimhe seo faoi thoibreacha beannaithe. Is é a chuir na saothair i dtoll a chéile.

St Bride's Inn well, Little Haven, Pembrokeshire, digitally married with an image of St Bridget from Ireland

Cyflwyniad
Introduction
Réamhrá

One of the earliest and most significant connections between Ireland and Wales is to be found within the diverse incidences of our sacred springs and holy wells, and the saints and practices that developed around them. This is nowhere more strong than in the associations between Pembrokeshire and County Wexford.

There are powerful historical links between St David *(Dewi Sant)* and St Aidan *(Maedog, Mogue* or *Madoc)* of Ferns, the latter having been trained by the former. There are churches dedicated to David in County Wexford (Oilgate, Mulrankin, Davidstown); and to Aidan in Pembrokeshire (Solva, Llawhaden, Nolton, Haroldston West). And *'Maen Dewi'* (or David's Stone) – a rock which may have been of spiritual significance to the earliest of our ancestors and upon which a Christian ring-cross was later carved – sits today, appropriately perhaps, in the porch of one of Aidan's Pembrokeshire churches, in Upper Solva.

Both saints have important holy well sites in both counties and countries. These include Ffynnon Faiddog at Whitesands Bay near St Davids, and St Mogue's Well at Ferns; and St David's Well at Oilgate in County Wexford, and Ffynnon Dewi (the probable place of David's baptism) at Porthclais in Pembrokeshire. In addition, there's the dramatically situated St Non's Well, at the site of Dewi's birth, as well as the many other wellspring sites named for saints revered on both sides of the Irish Sea, including St Bridget (Bride, or *San Ffraid* in Wales) at Artrama Castle, Tintern Abbey, Courtown and Brideswell Big in County Wexford, and Little Haven in Pembrokeshire; and those dedicated to the Virgin Mary at Maenclochog, Warren, Burton and Haverfordwest in Pembrokeshire, and Blackhall and Lady's Island in County Wexford.

And we shouldn't forget that St Patrick himself, the patron saint of the whole of Ireland, was probably Welsh! A resident (perhaps) of Banwen in the Dulais Valley, he was apparently first taken across the sea by pirates at the age of sixteen, then after six years as a slave managed to escape and return to his family in Wales, before being sent back to Ireland as a missionary in 432 AD.

It was our geographical proximity that most influenced the spread of Christianity from Wales to Ireland (and, importantly, back again), and from south-west Wales in particular. *Ard Ladrann*, thought to be modern-day Ardamine, near Courtown in northern County Wexford, or Beggerin Island, or Glascarrig Point, or Carnsore Point south of Rosslare (known as *Hieron Akron* / 'The Sacred Cape') are the probable first landing places of priests from south Wales, eager to spread the word. Their journeys, though never easy in the flimsy crafts on which they set sail, were at least relatively short. Just forty-odd miles across the Irish Sea from the site of St David's earliest monastery, they would have arrived with a mixture of relief and expectation onto the shores of the then mainly pagan lands of what we now know of as County Wexford.

· · ·

Poetry is one of the most powerful tools we have for the expression of our feelings, and the wellsprings of both Ireland and Wales have from earliest times inspired, confused and angered our writers. Their records are some of our best sources for understanding what these watery places meant to our ancestors.

As far back as the first century AD, the Roman Stoic philosopher, Seneca wrote that "where a spring rises … there should we build altars and offer sacrifices"; while 'The Mabinogion' – the earliest of our Welsh prose writings, compiled in the twelfth to thirteenth century from ancient traditional tales – warns that "Oni elli di ddiogelu'r ffynnon, ni elli ddiogelu'r deyrnas." (*Unless you can defend the well, you cannot defend your kingdom.* [Sioned Davies trans., 2007])

Irish writer Denis Devlin in his poem 'Encounter' recommends listening to "the world's / Growth, rustling in fire and childlike water!"; while nineteenth-century English nature poet, John Clare tells us in his 'Love and Memory' that "The nearer the fountain / More pure the stream flows".

In 'At Gumfreston Church' (printed in full on pages 18–19), Welsh poet Tony Curtis defines the three wellsprings below St Laurence's Church in Pembrokeshire as "Water that plays the oldest music", a title I have borrowed (with the writer's permission) for this small collection. Our wellspring sites throughout Wales and Ireland hold our deepest histories … in liquid form … bubbling and flowing from their constant though ever-changing presences as pagan sacred springs, 'christianised' as holy wells, some then transformed into medicinal spas, and beyond, right up to today.

These are the final few lines of 'An Tobar' / 'The Well' by Cathal Ó Searcaigh, a poet writing in the Ulster dialect of the Irish language (translated here by Frank Sewell). They both mourn the loss of so many of our original domestic springs while also powerfully asserting their continued importance for a focused and fulfilled life … especially in times of struggle and confusion:

"Is doiligh tobar a aimsiú faoi láthair,"
arsa Bríd, ag líonadh an bhabhla athuair.
"Tá siad folaithe i bhfeagacha agus i bhféar,
tachtaithe ag caileannógach agus cuiscreach,
ach in ainneoin na neamhairde go léir
níor chaill siad a dhath den tseanmhianach.
Aimsigh do thobar féin, a chroí,
óir tá am an anáis romhainn amach:
Cathfear pilleadh arís ar na foinsí."

(Bríd once said, / "It's hard to find a well these days", / as she filled up another bowl. / "They're hidden in bulrushes and grass, / choked by weeds and green scum / but for all the neglect, they've lost / not a drop of their true essence. / Find your own well, my lad, / for the arid times to come: / They dry up who steer clear of sources.")

But despite the apparent amnesia we have developed for many of our wellspring stories and the sad neglect of many of the sites themselves, it is clear that these ancient natural sources are still capable of providing inspiration, and especially to us writers and artists, offering portals into the past as well as answers, perhaps, to questions we haven't yet been able to fully articulate.

• • •

In his 1917 play, *At the Hawk's Well* (based upon the tales of Cuchulain, the mythological hero of ancient Ulster), WB Yeats posed a question: "Who but an idiot would praise dry stones in a well?".

It turns out that the answer is quite a lot of us. This collection, sitting alongside the growing interest in our natural water sources and the importance of these ancient locations in making sense of and giving meaning to our lives, suggests that a growing number of people are once again making visits to these often out-of-the-way places, still happy to praise our wellspring sites, even those with only "dry stones" on show. In this publication, poems from our deep, shared pasts, as well as new works by contemporary poets following in earlier footsteps and tracing the pen strokes of earlier writers on both sides of the Irish Sea are on offer, and in an imaginative dialogue with my own new photographic responses.

The final few words, then, must go to a poet, one of our greatest, Ireland's and the world's Seamus Heaney. These are his apparently simple though profound lines placed here into the mouths of the chorus of his 1990 verse play (based upon Sophocles' 'Philoctetes'), *The Cure at Troy*:

So hope for the great sea-change
On the far side of revenge.
Believe that a further shore
Is reachable from here.
Believe in miracles,
And cures and holy wells.

The single well structure that remains at Nine Wells, near Solva, Pembrokeshire

St Munn's Well, Browncastle, near Taghmon, County Wexford

Y Cerddi
The Poems
Na Dánta

The first poem in this short collection details a visit to St Non's Well and St David's Cathedral. It was written by **Lewys Glyn Cothi** [c.1420–90] about the pilgrimage of one Edudful ferch Gadwgon and her sons, as part of *A Mother Prays to St Non, St David and the Rood of Chester*. It is thought to be the oldest-known account of a visit to St Non's.

During medieval times, the shrine of St David in Pembrokeshire was one of the most popular destinations for pilgrims, possessing as it did the relics of the saint. Two pilgrimages to St Davids was equal to one to Rome, and one of the highlights of any visit would have been the short walk from the town and its cathedral to the place where David was born. His mother was St Non (also known as Nonna or Nonnita) and the ruins of her chapel and her well, overlooking St Non's Bay are still, today, popular pilgrimage destinations for people of all faiths and none. Said to have been raped by the ironically named Sanctus, a king of Ceredigion, David's coming into the world was a difficult one within a thunder and lightning storm, the well said to have burst forth at the moment when he emerged from his mother's womb.

The poem is written in the traditional Welsh *cywydd deuair hirion* (or *cywydd* for short) praise-verse form of seven syllable lines, rhyming couplets (one rhyme accented, one not), and the complex system of alliteration, consonance and internal rhyme known as *cynghanedd* (meaning 'harmony'):

Edudful Dduwsul a ddaw
a Dduw i wir weddiaw;
bwrw ei phwys yn eglwys Non,
bwrw ei phen lle bo'r ffynnon,
dyrchaf dwylaw yn llawen,
addoli oll i'r ddelw wen,
ennyn y cwyr melyn mawr,
a'i roi olla r yr allawr;
oddyno heibio'dd â hi
i glos da eglwys Dewi;
Offrymu, cusanu'r sant,
ddo gyr rhudd ac ariant.

(On Sunday Edudful comest / to pray sincerely to God; / she visits Non's church, / puts her head in the well / raises her hands merrily, / worships the holy image, / lights the large, yellow candles, / and puts all of them on the altar; / from there she passes to / the good close of St David's church; / Makes an offering of crimson wax / and silver and kisses the saint.)

This is the account from 'Betha Máedócc Ferna' (The Life of Maedoc of Ferns) of the genesis of Aidan's well at Ferns, conjured by the saint himself when local people building his great monastery complained of not having any water to drink. His first instruction was to "dig at the root of yonder tree …":

Uiscce ar tosach na tennta
Ni frith a fFerna roimhe,
Gur muigh a bun an bhile
Topar fa gile gloine.

Tiopra Maodhócc go maisi
Ainm na glaisi go gnathach,
Biaidh os gach uiscce iodhan
Sreabn na tiopra gan tragadh.

(At the beginning of the effort no water / Was found at Ferns, / Till there burst forth from the root of the tree / A fount clearer than crystal. //

Beautiful spring of Macdoc / Is the usual name of the brook, / Above every (other) pure water / The stream of the fountain will never ebb.)

Lewis Glyn Cothi [1420–1490] described St David as "penitent at the fountain's edge". This is twelfth-century poet **Gwynfardd Brycheiniog** on Dewi Sant's many churches and holy wells:

Dewi differwys ei eglwysau,
Dichones rhag gormes gormant greiriau
A ffynnawn Ddewi a'i ffynhonnau-llawn,
Llawer un rhadlawn, ffrwythlawn ffrydau.

(Dewi guarded his churches, / He built powerful defences against oppression / As well as Dewi's spring and his bubbling wells / Many of them full of grace, fruitful sources.)

And this is from 'The Life of St David' by **Ieuan ap Rhydderch** [c.1430–1470]:

Yn Eglwys y Groes oesir
Y ganed hwn, ganiad hir.
Pan esgores y pennaeth,
Y llech yn ddwylech ydd aeth.

Duw wrth fedyddiaw Dewi
A wnaeth ffons o ddwfr i ni.

(In the ancient Church of the Holy Cross / This man was born, a lengthy chant. / When she gave birth to the leader, / The stone broke into two stones. // When David was baptised, / God made a fount of water for us.)

This *cywydd* by an unrecorded medieval author writing about the Virgin Mary contains the wonderful lines:

Mal yr haul y molir hon
Drwy ffenestr wydr i'r ffynnon.

(She is worshipped like the sun / Passing through a glass window to the fountain.)

A WELL IN PEMBROKESHIRE / A WELL IN WEXFORD

This one is the pupil of an eye.
It exists to gaze at heaven.
Even the winter snows
kiss it and leave; no ice
forms here, for the pulse at its core
keeps its sight clear.
My face, hovering, it knows
will pass; all shadows do.
Only the sky endures.

And this one is a summery mirror
avid for something to reflect
branches, birds, our gawping –
and it giggles, when anything touches it,
shiggling out a little overflow.
All on the surface? The reverse.
The negative of every image
is banked and catalogued in its vault.

These wells hear the sea that roils between them.
Like siblings in the dark, they reach
for one another's hand
far below the boisterous tides
and spell on each other's fingers
all they have seen and understood.

We think it is we who do
the looking. When the time approaches
for the world to blister, God
will command that everything be screened;
that the wells, erupting, stream
the banners of their spoils. We'll see
ourselves, forever at the brink.

Angela Graham

St Cooraun's Blessed Well, near Enniscorthy, County Wexford

AT GUMFRESTON CHURCH

That evening, after a hard, hot drive,
The dark lane's coolness of trees
Was like water walked into,
Calm and quiet – no traffic,
Deep shadows,
All the gulls out at sea.

Augustus and Gwen's father
Walked the two miles from Tenby
Every Sunday to play the organ here.
I search for his headstone and find no-one
But Ken Handicott the grocer
I worked for one school summer holiday
Forty years ago.

They leave the church door unlocked:
There is no congregation but the curious passing folk.
And inside is the simple splendour of stone font,
Low wooden roof, draped altar, Norman-built
On earlier significance – St Teilo, St Bridget.
The place shivers in the dusk
And moves into another night.

Here were the early missions, saints and sinners
Crossing the Irish Sea, moving east
With their crosses and swords.
Here was a quay, a village the river Ritec
Joined to the sea that led to the world.
And here, behind the church, before the woods
Where the Magdalens brought their lepers,
Still flow the three springs of purity
And healing, coming to us from a depth.

St Lawrence Church, Gumfreston, near Tenby, Pembrokeshire

Water that plays the oldest music.
Without thinking
I take a handful
And with wet, cool fingers
Cross myself.

Tony Curtis

Blessed Well, Ballincoola, County Wexford

BLESSED WELLS

Blessed are the wells
where water flowed or flows.
Heavenly, divine and hopeful
filled with belief and miraculous wonder
these saintly-named wells signify
much more than meets the eye.

Walking up or down moss-grown steps
towards a wishing well, a living well,
stepping stones upon sacred grounds,
holy water representing purity
and deliverance from evil,
from Satan's Hell flames.

Fire and water strong against ground rock,
the homeopathic healing qualities of a drop.
Water memories connecting all
from pilgrims to historians, writers,
any visitor travelling from near or far.
A living well gives the gift of life.

A spring helps to keep you
balanced and strong,
rock solid to live well.

Grace O'Reilly

BEDYDDIO DEWI

Yn harbwr Porth Clais y mae afon Alun
Yn llifo i'r môr. A stori'n ei dilyn.

Yma, medde nhw, (er does neb yn cofio)
Y cafodd Dewi Sant ei fedyddio.

Rhyw fynach dall oedd yn dal y bachgen
I'w drochi'n lân dros ei ben a'i dalcen.
Ac wrth iddo'i ollwng i ganol y tonnau
A'i godi drachefn â nerth ei freichiau
Fe dasgodd y dŵr ar draws ei wyneb.

Agorodd ei lygaid yn llawn o ddisgleirdeb.

A gwelodd, am y tro cyntaf erioed,
Y blodau ar gloddiau a'r dail ar y coed,
A gweled yr afon yn troelli drwy'r pant:
Diolchodd o'i galon i'r bachgen o sant.

Ymhen blynyddoedd, ar ôl tyfu'n ŵr,
Nid oedd Dewi yn yfed dim ond dŵr,
Ac fe aeth ar ei siwrnai ar draws y wlad
I ddweud wrth y bobol fod Duw inni'n Dad,
Eu dysgu i weddïo, a maddau i elyn,
Cyn dod yn ôl i fyw yng Nglyn Rhosyn.

Ar ôl i Dewi i dyfu'n ddyn
Mae'n wir, fe agorodd e lygaid sawl un.

Eirwyn George

*Cerdd syml i blant. Seiliwyd ar y traddodiad i Dewi Sant gael ei fedyddio ym
Mhorth Clais, ar bwys Tyddewi. Yn ôl y chwedl, cafodd y mynach dall oedd
yn ei ddal ei olwg am y tro cyntaf ar ôl i'r dŵr dasgu ar ei wyneb.*

St Aidan's Cathedral, Enniscorthy, County Wexford

BAPTISING DEWI

At Porth Clais harbour the river Alun
Flows into the sea. Followed by a story.

Here, so they say (though nobody remembers)
Dewi Sant was baptised.

A blind monk was holding the boy
Ready to be immersed in the flowing river,
And as he lowered him in the midst of the waves
And lifted him again with all the might of his arms
The water splashed over his face.

He opened his eyes which were full of splendour and brilliance.

And he saw for the first time in his life
The flowers on the hedgerows and the leaves on the trees,
And the river winding its way to the sea.
He gave the saintly boy the thanks that he felt in his heart.

In a few years' time, when a grown-up man,
Dewi drank nothing but water;
And he travelled around the country
To tell the people that God was our Father.
He taught them to pray, and to forgive their enemies,
Before he came back to live in Glyn Rhosyn.

It is true to say
that he opened the eyes of many.

Eirwyn George

*A simple poem for children based on the tradition that Dewi Sant
was baptised at Porth Clais, near St Davids. According to the legend
the blind monk who held him was able to see for the first time when
the water splashed on his face.*

FFYNNON TREMARCHOG

Gwrandewch ar barablu'r swigod o berfedd ein daear
Crochan bywyd i genedlaethau di-ri
Llysiau'r dyfroedd, perlysiau'r ddôl a'n cyndeidiau ni
O'u swyn elfennol daw heddwch i mi.

Dyfroedd fu'n pefrio cyn oes y gaer
A theyrnas dros feini Carrian a'i lu
Meini sy'n nodi y gwanwyn a ddaw
Yn gadarn eu hôl er milenia a fu.

I ddilynwyr y Grêd yn y llan ar y bryn
Dyma oedd ffynnon bedydd y fro
I'r ffydd oesol, cyn geni ein Sant
Yn fendith i bawb, pwy bynnag y bo.

Ffynnon sicr ei llif i ddiwallu pob gofyn
Cenedlaethau o blant a theuluoedd y fro
Wedi diffodd tanau simdde, helem a gwair
A galw sawl milwr fu'n gwarchod y fro.

Wrth gofio am glebran foreol morwynion
Tra'n casglu llond stên o ddŵr risial y Ffynnon
Diolchaf o'm calon, am y cysur a leddfa
Niferus anghenion trigolion ein pentra.

Anonymous

A found poem about the holy well at Tremarchog / St Nicholas, with a translation on the next page by **Dafydd Williams** *who lives near Ffynnon Tremarchog.*

FFYNNON TREMARCHOG

Listen … chattering bubbles sing from our Mother Earth
Innumerable generations have sprung from your womb
Our forebears, our plants, of meadow and rill
This elemental song brings solace to me.

Her waters have sparkled for aeons of time
Ages uncounted before castle and Carrian
Unknown prince whose mark still notes
The seasons that rule both your life and mine.

In the millennia before Dewi our Saint
And all Christians of the church on the hill
Did they also take their blessings, whoever they were
From this Spring of Life that is so near.

Our spring, its unending flow, that satisfies all
Generations of children, all families in need
Extinguisher of fires, chimney and farm
The needs of the military when guarding our land.

Listen … the morning chatter as housemaids all
Collect their daily churns of crystal life
From our hearts give thanks for the succour to all
That ease their troubles at our Spring of Life.

Dafydd Williams (translator)

ST GOVAN'S CHAPEL AND WELL

The hermitage
an over-sized mollusc,
is stuck on limestone
where starkness has taken hold
and sprouts
like grass,
the sea, the wind and itinerant sun
conjoin in a seasonless pact
to scour
and pare back.

So prayer
becomes elemental too,
stripped of nuance or detail
without even the clutter of words,
the rough walls
cradle the buffeted stillness
as if a new-born flame.

This cleave of rock
disrupting the imperious cliff
prises space,
St Govan's Chapel consecrating
a pooling
of the westward flow of time.

Julian Cason

Over: St Govan's Wells, near Bosherston, Pembrokeshire. Govan was either
the sixth-century Gobhan of Wexford, or even Gwain of Arthurian fame.

Bride's Cross in St Bridget's Well, Courtown, County Wexford

THE WATER IS WITHIN ME

The pool is still and quiet.
On my approach,
it almost seems to tease.
It scorns my troubled mind with
a noiseless reproach.
I sit and drop my hand into the portal.

Ice cold, it bites ... but ...
thoughts and fears and doubts
tumble and toss about my head
mundane, uncommon,
unworldly, supernatural.
The water works its magic
and I sit.

I rip my petticoat and whisper
entreaties into the woven fabric,
dip it deep into the waters
– Goddess hear me now –
and tie it to the closest bough.
I stand and smile,
blessed,
and walk away.

I am still now, and quiet
– the water is within me.
My troubles are washed away.

Lorraine O'Dwyer

*A response to three of Bridget's wells in County Wexford
at Tintern, Courtown and Brideswell Big.*

MANY WELLS, ONE WATER

Many wells, one water,
life creator, sustainer,
flowing through all beings,
a cycle of birth and rebirth
used, then purified.

In primordial seas
life's journeys began.
Listen to our story,
its flow.
Water synonymous with life.

In St Nicholas parish,
water was gifted to the village
by a natural spring,
part of a global waterweb
since the most ancient of times,

the village gathered,
a blackbird welcomed the morning,
pails fetching up.
From the 'boiling' sand
the clear water, purified.

Around the well,
laughter and gossip shared.
What's essential replenished
for our watery nature.
Living water, purified.

In an age of flick a switch,
turn on a tap,
it's too easy to forget.
Remember our life journey
and our sacred wells.

Brian Jackson

Ffynnon Tremarchog / St Nicholas' Well, St Nicholas, near Fishguard,
Pembrokeshire

St Garvan's Well, Carrowreagh, near Taghmon, County Wexford

SOMETIMES CURSE, SOMETIMES CURE

To sometimes curse, more often cure,
For those who watch and wait
Belief conjoins with magic
To throb with faith – and hate.

To sometimes curse, more often cure,
Wild water drives out pain
While placid streams soothe troubled dreams,
The water and the wells remain.

To sometimes curse, more often cure,
There is a power in the play
Of holy water coursing
Over limestone beds of grey.

To sometimes curse, more often cure,
Down pilgrim ways profound,
The souls of long-dead searchers stay
For this is holy ground.

Phil Carradice

St David's Baptismal Well, Porthclais, Pembrokeshire

TELLING THE BEES: a tale of two wells

Sitting close together by
Porthclais's ancient sacred spring,
young Aidan was enquiring of his master
what he should take back to Ireland,
what best would remind him of
his time in Wales, when
an answer settled on the old man's
bare arm, a honey bee,
mistaking the gentle sweetness of
his unwashed skin
for the fragrance of a flower.

*

Apis mellifera, the western honey bee
from age-old hives in Egypt where
its nectar was the food of gods,
Tutankhamun and his kin attended
by a larder of essential jars
filled to the brim and set beside
his gold and jewelled sarcophagus,
in prudent preparation for
the unsure journey
to another world.

*

Designed perfect as powder puffs
for pollen hunting,
these agents of the buzz offer their
essential service, free of charge,
their long proboscides sucking up
the nectar's sugary waters,
conveying its syrupy dna from
flowers' male to female organs.
And to communicate locations of
the best new plants in bloom,
the bees perform their moonwalk-ballet,

their angled-accurate 'waggle dance'
back to their hard-working sisters in the nest
through internal clock and
solar compass choreography.

In Aidan's day (as well before),
these tiny hallowed insects
had the quiet powers of prophesy,
seers into what was to come,
and faithful interpreters of
the confusions of what had
already been.

We even used to 'tell the bees' when
someone died or, replacing those fallen,
a child was born,
while also whispering news of
all betrothals and marriages,
of all the long and perilous journeys
needing to be made.

And as the bees were
messengers between
the living and the dead,
you'd never ever quarrel
in hearing distance of
a nest or hive.

I'm stung by all of this!
*
So, when arriving with
his gently humming cargo at
the rocky sweep of Ardamine Bay,
Aidan – on fire with holy pollen – was
the first, it's claimed, to sweeten Ireland
with Welsh honey,

walking his new ideas from
this flower to the next,
his bees secured and grown, back then,
in coiled wicker skeps,
plastered with dung and mud,

their six-sided wax-comb tessellations
models still for the geometry of
neighbourly home-building,
though smashed by man when harvesting
the honey from the hive.

*

What the bees find and collect
flavours our lives,
while still we raid the nests,
smoke out the hives to deaden
and subdue.

The sun is low
and there are no more giants here,
only the lengthening gloom of
small unimpressive men
casting drawn-out shadows through which
we're compelled to walk.

Who's able still to make us sweet, and
what's leaving that sour taste
in our mouths, today, when trees
at rag wells hung once with hopes to
banish pain and fear
are wreathed with dog-shit bags
in our new response to
ills and ignorance?

Is there a 'saint' of some description
who's ready to return

Dewi's ancient favour,
to reconstruct the shattered hive,
uncrack the egg,
place back the serpent stone upon the stone,
to teach us how and when to use
the older names, and how
to dance together once again
in circles and in figures-of-eight
around this flower, on to the next,
to tell, in quiet apologetic tones,
our sad new tales to the bees?

*

Let's end the quarrel, then,
and light our beeswax candles
against the dark,
drink our mead, and ring
what little's left today of Aidan's Bell,
as Aidan did
beside his well at Ferns
before the call came loud and clear
(via humming messengers, perhaps?)
from ailing David
approaching now his end
to visit him in Wales, for one last time,
and Aidan went, of course,
swiftly back across
the often-worrying waters with
his brightest token of
what flowered best between them,
what scented both their lives and
both their peoples' lands,
reminding of their real shared treasure,
beeswax sealed within
a single tiny pot.

Phil Cope

St Non's Well, near St Davids, Pembrokeshire

Biographies

Phil Cope is a writer, photographer, and exhibition and book designer on a wide range of subjects from Haitian vodou to the Spanish Civil War, from the singer, actor and activist Paul Robeson to the footballer John Charles, from the prehistory of Margam Park to the Olympic and Paralympic Games, in addition to his celebrated series of books on Welsh, Cornish, Scottish and English sacred springs and holy wells. Born in Cardiff, and after travelling extensively throughout Europe, North, Central and South America, the Middle East and Asia, he now lives at the dead-end of an ex-coalmining valley, the subject of his most recent publication, The *Golden Valley: a visual biography of the Garw*. He is currently working on a major new illustrated volume on the wells of Ireland, and a book of narrative poems and photographs on wellspring sites and their stories from around the world.

Lewys Glyn Cothi [c. 1420–90] was born in Llanybydder in south-west Wales. He was one of the most prominent itinerant 'Poets of the Nobility' *(Beirdd yr Uchelwyr).*

Gwynfardd Brycheiniog was a twelfth-century Welsh 'Court Poet', noted in particular for his eulogies in praise of Dewi Sant. His name suggests that he was a native of Brecon.

Ieuan ap Rhydderch [c. 1430–1470] was an important collector of ancient Welsh manuscripts, as well as 'a gentleman and poet of Cardiganshire'.

Angela Graham is from Belfast. A fluent Welsh-speaker, she has been a film-maker in Wales for decades. Seren Books published her poetry collection *Sanctuary: There Must Be Somewhere* in May 2022, and her debut collection of short stories *A City Burning* in 2020, which was long-listed for the Edge Hill Prize.

Tony Curtis is Emeritus Professor of Poetry at the University of South Wales. He grew up in Pembrokeshire where his family farmed and mined for over two centuries. He has written extensively about west Wales, including *Real South Pembrokeshire* in the *Seren Real Wales* series. His next collection, *Leaving the Hills*, is his eleventh and includes new poems inspired by the west of Wales. He has recently published his first novel, *Darkness in the City of Light*, set in wartime Paris.

Grace O'Reilly is a published poet and writer, both in print and online, who resides in Gorey, County Wexford with her husband and two children. Grace is a regular book reviewer for writing.ie, as well as other platforms, and is a member of several writing groups and book clubs.

Eirwyn George, born in 1936, was a secondary school teacher and activities librarian in Pembrokeshire before retiring in 1990. He won the Crown twice at the National Eisteddfod and has published twenty-two volumes of poetry and prose. He and his wife live in Maenclochog, Pembrokeshire.

Dafydd Williams has lived in Tremarchog (or St Nicholas) for more than eighty years, bar interruptions for his agricultural education in Carmarthenshire and Devon, and two years working at the University of Nottingham, before he returned to run a farm and take over the village shop.

Julian Cason lives in Cardiff. His professional life has been mainly spent working with the terminally ill. He has been published in *Envoi, Pulp Poets Press, Nine Muses, The Dawn Treader, Black Bough Poetry, Bindweed,* and *Full House* (Featured Creator), *Ink Drinkers, The Frogmore Papers* and *Sarasvati*, and long-listed for the Cinnamon Press Literature Award 2022.

Lorraine O'Dwyer has been a practicing Pagan for over thirty years. She works as the Gallivanting Folklore and Foraging guide in the woodlands surrounding her home in County Wexford. She is the latest in a long line of *'bean feasa'* or wise women in her family, and proudly carries on this tradition of lending support, medicine and wisdom to her community.

Brian Jackson has lived in Llandruidion Farm, Pencaer, near Fishguard for the past twenty-one years. He is interested in green spirituality, celebrating our connection with the past, all beings and our sacred land. He doesn't claim to be a poet – his training was in electrical engineering ending up in senior management – although he has had a few poems published. He is a member of Fishguard Arts Society.

Phil Carradice is a poet, novelist and historian who comes from Pembrokeshire but lives, now, in the Vale of Glamorgan. He has written over fifty books and is a regular broadcaster on TV and radio. His most recent book, *Keeping the Home Fires Burning,* is a study of how morale was maintained in the First World War. He is currently working on a book about witchcraft and witch hunting.

Diolchiadau
Mae fy nyled i'n fawr i Dr Robin Gwyndaf, Darren Dobbs, R Iestyn Daniel, Stephen Thomas, a'r holl feirdd a ysgrifennodd weithiau newydd i'r gyfrol hon neu a gynigiodd gynnwys gwaith a oedd eisoes yn bodoli.
Phil Cope

Acknowledgements
I am indebted for the assistance in pulling this short collection together to Dr Robin Gwyndaf, Darren Dobbs, R Iestyn Daniel, Stephen Thomas, and all of the poets who wrote new works for this book or offered the inclusion of existing ones.
Phil Cope

Nóta buíochais
Tá mé faoi chomaoin ag na daoine seo a leanas as an gcúnamh chun an cnuasach seo a chur le chéile: Dr Robin Gwyndaf, Darren Dobbs, R Iestyn Daniel, Stephen Thomas, agus na filí go léir a scríobh saothair nua nó a chuir saothair a scríobhadh cheana ar fáil le haghaidh an leabhair. Phil Cope

Testun **Text** Téacs Phil Cope

Barddoniaeth **Poems** Dánta
Gweithiau hen a newydd gan **Old and new works by** Saothair, idir shean agus nua, le:
Lewys Glyn Cothi, Gwynfardd Brycheiniog, Ieuan ap Rhydderch, Angela Graham, Tony Curtis, Grace O'Reilly, Eirwyn George, Dafydd Williams, Julian Cason, Lorraine O'Dwyer, Brian Jackson, Phil Carradice, Phil Cope

Ffotograffau **Photographs** Grianghraif Phil Cope

Dylunio **Design** Dearadh Heidi Baker